JOAN
OF ARC

⚜

Maid of Orléans

JOAN OF ARC

Maid of Orléans

JEANETTE STRUCHEN

Franklin Watts, Inc.
575 Lexington Avenue
New York, New York 10022

Cover photograph courtesy
The Bettmann Archive

Map by Dyno Lowenstein

CONTENTS

CONTENTS

JOAN
OF ARC

⚜

Maid of Orléans

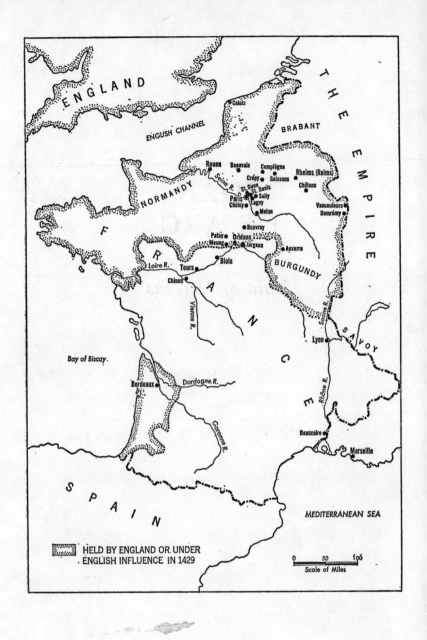

ENGLAND

ENGLISH CHANNEL

THE EMPIRE

BRABANT

Calais

NORMANDY

Rouen
Beauvais
Crépy
Compiègne
Soissons
Rheims (Reims)
Châlons

Seine R.

St. Ouen
St. Denis
Sully
Paris
Choisy
Lagny
Melun

Vaucouleurs
Domrémy

F
R
A
N
C
E

Rouvray

Patay
Meung
Orléans
Jargeau
Auxerre

Loire R.
Tours
Blois

BURGUNDY

Chinon

Vienne R.

Saône R.

SAVOY

Lyon

Bay of Biscay

Bordeaux
Dordogne R.

Garonne R.

Rhône R.

Beaucaire

Marseille

SPAIN

MEDITERRANEAN SEA

HELD BY ENGLAND OR UNDER
ENGLISH INFLUENCE IN 1429

0   50   100
Scale of Miles

CHAPTER ONE

CRUCIFIXION BY FIRE

⚜⚜⚜⚜ "HAND me a cross. Please hand me a cross," murmured the maid Joan, as her bare feet mounted the hastily cut logs now stacked for the burning of a witch. Some of the logs rolled under the weight of her body, but no one braced her against falling. There was no escape. Indeed, these final steps were symbolic of her life's mission. The way had been rough and uphill, but she had never expected it to be easy—only successful.

Joan had long ago run out of fear; she could not remember when. Maybe it was the day that she left her parents at Domrémy for the first time, or when the commander at Vaucouleurs gave her a horse and armor to visit her exiled king. When fear had disappeared, it had left in its stead a mighty sense of direction toward victory. But was this her victory? Was victory this brush pile stacked to burn her alive?

A crowd was gathering. Some were soldiers holding battle swords as if they were ready to ransack the entire French city of Rouen. These tall and strong figures made the maid in white seem even smaller. Their heads were covered with helmets, and the sun's rays sparkled on their coats of mail, which, in turn, threw dancing beams of light across the wood, giving the illusion that the igniting of the logs had already taken place.

Several men slung extra wood onto the mound and joked nervously, as others tested the firmness of the stake.

Some of the crowd hung back, not knowing whether to sympathize or to ridicule. Their indecision was the same response that Joan had always known; one minute the people were with her, the next, against her.

With effort, the nineteen-year-old girl reached the top of the mound, and a heavy hand backed her to the stake. There was no conversation, no tears, no recanting. The crowd was more restless than the victim. Emotion hung in the air, almost touchable.

"Hand me a cross. Please hand me a cross." The request was made once again, but a cross did not come forth.

Joan's eyes lifted to the blue May sky as she felt the rope binding her body to the wooden stake. It had been such a short ride in the cart from the clammy, dark prison, and she tried to forget the walls which had been meant to press her into a confession. She tried to forget the grueling hours, days, weeks of questions, when self-proclaimed authorities paced before her in their regal costumes, waving documents which awaited her signature.

2

The ropes were pulled tight, and they held her body rigid against a post that had once grown strong as part of a living tree. It had been fed from within as she had been fed from within. It had once had roots as she had had roots, and now, together, their ashes would mingle and take on a new form.

Had her crime been so unforgivable? She had honored her father and mother. She had not been a thief. She had not committed adultery. She had loved the Lord God with her whole soul, and because of her love she had led France to victory over the English enemy. The king was on his throne, and she had been ready to go home after the coronation, but her fate had taken her through days of inquisition, and now this.

The crowd edged closer, and windows opened from buildings on the square as onlookers perched themselves on windowsills. The whole world seemed to be staring as it had stared months before when the people had hailed her last military victory.

The ropes hurt her waist where the prison chains had rubbed, and her wrists and ankles were beginning to ache as the numbness wore off.

When the ropes were tied securely, a soldier placed a paper cap on her head. She knew from the voices in the mob that it bore the words "Heretic, Relapse, Apostate, Idolator."

The prisoner could scarcely move. Certainly she could not jump from the mound of wood as she had jumped

3

from the sixty-foot tower trying to escape her imprisonment before coming to Rouen. She had lost all hope that the king of France, for whom she had fought, would pay a ransom and save her from the stake. But she had not lost hope that in this dark hour her two saints and the Archangel Michael would rescue her soul. It was in this faith that her lips started to move, and those nearby could hear her gentle prayer of forgiveness for the king, her enemies, those who condemned her, and those who readied the fire.

Then, above all, came the voice of a judge, who listed twelve accusations, one by one. As the list grew, his powerful voice excited the crowd, and the low murmuring took on such an intense volume that Joan wondered whether anyone in all of France had been on her side. The judge shouted that she had worn boy's clothing; that she had heard voices; and that she was a heretic of the church. He reminded the crowd of her bold predictions of victory at Orléans. He reminded them of her ego when she had vowed that she was in a state of God's grace. Above all, he shouted her prediction that the Dauphin would rule France again and drive the English home.

When the judge had rolled up his document and had moved back into the crowd, Pierre Cauchon, Joan's main accuser, read the sentence. He read it not to the ever-growing mob, but to Joan the Maid.

How often she had heard his demanding voice: "Sign."

"Recant." How often she had seen his wizardry against her. As bishop of Beauvais, was he not out of his legal territory in this trial? Yet he had handpicked sixty judges who would yield to his desires and kill the girl who had hurled her voices and visions at the church. During the trial Joan had watched him command the scribes to take down only those statements which accused her of heresy, and order them to ignore those which would prove her case. She was allowed no defense but her own, and she suspected that Cauchon had bribed the five guards to threaten her with tortures. These threats kept her sleepless night after night.

Now this stake was the climax of her ordeal.

When Father Ladvenu heard her confession and gave her the sacrament before she left the prison for the market square, he thought again that men were committing a terrible error against this girl. He knew that a witch would have pleaded for mercy, but Joan's undaunted courage must prove the existence of special authority.

"Away with her!" snapped the magistrate.

"A cross. Please, a cross."

Quickly an English soldier, a member of the enemy ranks, twisted two sticks together and handed them up to where Joan stood. Then, behind the pressing crowd, the voice of Isambard de la Pierre begged the mob to let him through, and he appeared with a cross from the Church of Saint Saviour.

"The fire! The fire has started," yelled the eager spectators, still not knowing whether to make this a joyful or a tragic event.

The black smoke rose, and the heat caused the crowd to move away. Isambard de la Pierre was fearful that Joan could not see the cross through the smoke and fire. Grabbing a soldier's spear, he raised the cross high, and Joan's eyes followed.

Her eyes had always followed the cross. Even in the parish of Domrémy, she had been known in childhood as a religious. She had followed the cross into every battle, to the coronation of the Dauphin in Rheims Cathedral, and to prison, and now she was following it to her death.

The crowd became quiet. Some people knelt as they watched a calm serenity engulf the burning girl.

"We have burned a witch," some insisted.

"No, we have burned a saint," came the reply.

Joan's whole life had been brittle kindling in the hands of her enemies. She was burned by traditions that kept girls illiterate and out of the public eye. She was burned by the religious practices of the day which let evil men go unchallenged. She was burned by church orthodoxy which freely labeled heretics and witches.

News traveled slowly in 1431, but as it spread throughout France that the stake had claimed Joan's life, the stirrings of belief in her immortality began. In the years that followed, it did not seem mere chance that her accusers, one by one, met with tragedies. With each tragedy the memory of Joan's courage grew stronger. Motivated by this memory, France drove out the English and built a new nation. Monuments to Joan dotted the land, and her deathday, rather than her birthday, was set apart for remembrance. Tales of her sainthood became as ordinary as lavender growing along the byways of France. Finally, she was canonized as a saint, and Joan of Arc took her place among the immortals of mankind.

✠ CHAPTER TWO ✠

REBEL WITH A CAUSE

✠✠✠✠ IT WAS a time, like times before and times after, when the rich got richer and the poor got poorer. It was a time of shaking foundations; a time of exiled queens, mad kings, and conniving nobles. It was a time when spies crept into inner circles, setting friend against friend and plot against plot. The rebellious were everywhere, and their hunger pangs roared in the ears of the powerful. Kings danced on political strings held by nobles, and nobles slept with one eye open, afraid of being stabbed by their servants.

Into this fifteenth-century world, Joan of Arc (Jeanne d'Arc) was born on January 6, 1412, in Domrémy Parish, Lorraine Province, France. Her parents, Jacques and Isabelle, were poor. To be poor is not a disgrace, but to be kept poor by political pressures turns paupers into warriors. Most families wanted to be loyal subjects of a French king, but the throne shifted between England and France after every major battle in what added up to the Hundred Years' War.

9

The young man who was to be king in Joan's lifetime was a prince on a string, who had inherited fifty years of war, foreign invaders, civil war, and national apathy. Without crown or power, Charles VII lived in a castle at Chinon on the Vienne River. He could not be crowned so long as most of France, including Paris and Rheims (now Reims), was under English rule. Also, there was some doubt as to whether he was the legitimate heir.

Joan's natural intelligence kept her aware of war issues. She watched the men of Domrémy leave home as young, brave recruits and come back old in body and spirit, if they came back at all. She watched the countryside blanching under pressures that drained its wealth and resources. She listened as agreements for temporary treaties were read publicly in the marketplace, and she thought about them as she watched her father's sheep or sewed beside her mother.

"What do you want, mother? I heard you call all the way from the field."

"I did not call. You must have heard the children playing."

Such a mistake seemed normal enough, and if anyone was normal it was this thirteen-year-old girl, racing through the fields with her friends. Battle games changed into gay-hearted rebellion when make-believe knights whisked away an imaginary crown from the head of a sleeping prince.

"Joan, you are a good child. You have been chosen to

help the king of France. You will do wonderful things for the King of Heaven."

"Hauriette, did you speak to me?" Joan asked her friend.

Hauriette shook her head.

Joan told no one of the voices that she heard. Like Mary, the Queen of Heaven, at her annunciation, "she kept all these things and pondered them in her heart."

For months Joan heard no voices at all, and finally she decided that they had left her forever. Then a voice commanded her to put on boys' clothing and join the army. It was so compelling that she was ready to leave that very minute, yet the shock of it left her immobile.

Later she heard a voice say, "Go to the captain at Vaucouleurs and direct him to give you an escort to see the Dauphin." Joan jumped to her feet at the very thought of doing such a thing. She reminded herself that such an action was for soldiers to undertake. She was a girl. She had no business before the king.

But the voice persisted. It gave her a sense of urgency. It gave her courage, and gave her direction.

One day Joan took her friend Hauriette by the hand and shared her experiences.

"Do you hear them all the time?" Hauriette asked.

"No, not all the time."

"Do they come when you are praying?"

"Sometimes—but just as often when I am not praying. I hear them when I am afraid to carry out God's command. I hear them when I am discouraged and feel like a girl who is dared to do something but has lost her nerve. I hear them when the time calls for action and my feet are standing still."

"Tell me again what the voices have said, Joan."

"They have said that I am a good girl. They have said that God has need of my arms and legs and head to do a great errand for Him. They have said that the Dauphin will be placed on the throne of France if I will put on boys' clothes and lead the army into victory against the English. They have said that I must go to the captain at Vaucouleurs and ask for an escort to the Dauphin."

"Oh, Joan, you're only a girl! It's wrong to pretend you are a boy, and"—Hauriette's voice became a whisper—"it's wrong to hear voices. They say only witches hear voices."

Tears rolled down Hauriette's cheeks, and fear drew her face into depths of sadness. Her shoulders began to shake, and she ran barefoot into the woods, sobbing all the way.

Joan's hardest task was to explain the voices to her parents, and their response was as she had expected. Her father said he would drown her with his own hands before he would let his daughter follow the army. Joan's mother, being more practical, said that Joan must forget these voices and begin to think of marriage and a family.

At last, rumors of Joan's voices spread throughout the town.

"There she goes! There's the girl who thinks she can save France," yelled a man who was pushing a cart of empty wine casks.

"Will you be queen?" taunted another.

"You know what they say about girls who follow the army!" an old man yelled, with laughter in his voice.

But Joan knew that she was not to follow the army; she was to lead it.

Through the summer heat of 1428, Joan listened to marriage plans being worked out by her parents. But so great was her confidence in the voices that she knew the boy who was intended as her husband would never be hers, and that the planned marriage was an empty scheme.

In December, 1428, Joan's uncle, Durand Lassois, came to Domrémy asking that Joan be allowed to go back to Vaucouleurs to help his wife with their new baby. Joan was ecstatic with joy. She saw this as a sign that the time had come for action. Her parents saw it as an opportunity for practical experience in child care now that Joan was preparing for marriage.

So Joan packed her belongings and put them in the cart that her uncle had brought.

With conviction in her soul, Joan bounced along the bumpy Burgundy road. Her enthusiasm burst into great surges of joy as she felt her mission about to unfold. The voices had said that she must see the Dauphin sometime during the middle of Lent in 1429, but it was several hundred miles from Vaucouleurs to Chinon and travel was slow.

The weeks passed quickly at Vaucouleurs, and one day Joan announced to her uncle, "I must go to the captain at the barracks today and tell him that a girl is to rally the French army and bring about the coronation of our king."

Knowing the tales of Joan's voices, Uncle Durand had been half aware that this day would come. With understanding eyes he nodded affirmatively.

Joan had been told explicitly by the voices, who identified themselves as the Archangel Michael, Saint Catherine, and Saint Margaret, exactly when to make her first public appearance.

The captain of the Vaucouleurs barracks was Robert de Baudricourt, a self-centered soldier who could change moods in the middle of a laugh.

"I have to see the Dauphin," Joan told him. "You must give me a horse and an escort to Chinon."

"Have you ever seen him?" asked the captain.

"No, sir, but I would know him anywhere and could pick him from a crowd of people. I am on an errand for God to crown the king."

Everyone had heard her plainly enough—the knight, the sergeants at arms, and the loose fringe of spectators. ". . . to crown the king." Suddenly the snickering stopped and the curious held their tongues. Everyone stared, and her words hung in the air.

14

"To crown the king, indeed! Box the girl's ears and send her home to her mother!"

At the captain's thundering order a tide of rocking laughter swept the people in the hall. The soldiers slapped each other on the back in jolly good sport over the crude answer to the country girl standing before them.

A strong hand grabbed Joan's arm and forced her to the door. But Joan walked through the heavy door with assurance that her cause was beyond the nearsightedness of those she had just met. The voices had not promised that the errand would be easy. She must try again.

For several days in her uncle's home, Joan reviewed what had happened, and she made up imaginary conversations, trying them out in her mind. Thoughts flowed like a raging river: "If I had said . . ." "If I had stood my ground when he said . . ." "If I had refused to leave when . . ." "If I had told him . . ."

Her thoughts were broken now and then by sounds of a familiar scene—well-armed soldiers ordering a group of ragged peasants to enter the military service. This scene remained in her mind as she planned her next visit to Captain Baudricourt.

Joan was perhaps the most insistent rebel that Robert de Baudricourt had ever met. Although he was convinced of her lunacy, he knew that not one of his men had ever shown such consistent, lasting determination for the cause of French victory.

"Today we have suffered another defeat near Orléans,

15

and haste in your decision to send me to the Dauphin is imperative," Joan said to the captain.

Baudricourt knew of no defeat, and he shook his head at her request for a horse and escort to see the prince at Chinon. Several hours later he shook his head again as he heard of the defeat from soldiers just back from Orléans.

Within the hour he called for Joan, and without apology offered her a horse and escort.

"She cannot go to the Dauphin in those rags," said a soldier.

"Neither can she ride as a girl following the army," said another.

Quickly, hose, jerkin, and doublet were gathered. Within twenty minutes Joan stood as straight and courageous as any soldier in all of France. Anyone could see that she was bright and intelligent, but little did they dream that within the next few years, this one girl would motivate an army, save a nation, and crown a king.

Captain Baudricourt ordered his handful of escorts to travel by night and guard against anyone seeing the girl. Perhaps he did not believe in this venture, but he kept remembering Joan's knowledge of the French defeat near Orléans.

Joan's cause was not to become a heroine. It was not to be the greatest military general that France had ever known. It was a single-minded obedience to God's command that she place the rightful king on his French throne and once again consolidate warring factions which had been split by the powerful nobility.

To be a rebel, one does not need followers, just a cause. A rebel does not stand on illusion but on belief and dedication—dedication strengthened by effort. Joan had to increase her effort because she appeared on the stage of history at a time when men wrote the script and played the leading roles. Girls were little more than domestic slaves. It was not surprising that soldiers laughed and nobility sneered at Joan's persistent statements about crowning the king and driving the English out. But by superior intelligence and natural leadership, Joan punched holes in the walls of fifteenth-century prejudices.

✠ CHAPTER THREE ✠

KING WITHOUT A COUNTRY

⚜⚜⚜ LIKE a game of checkers, the route taken by Joan and her escort to Chinon started in friendly territory, moved out to dodge the enemy, cautiously avoided capture, and aimed at crowning a king.

To reach Chinon meant two hundred and fifty miles and eleven days on horseback. Joan's escort watched especially for stray bandits who might come through the woods and kill them for provisions or run to warn the next town of approaching strangers. Such attention meant delay.

"What's that?"

Ears pitched to listen. They could not believe that many people of right intent would be walking at night in the dark, wet woods.

"I hear footsteps. Yes, we are not alone," the guards whispered. "Stand still. Do not breathe. Hold your horse on taut rein. Maybe it's an animal."

From no farther away than two hundred feet, the foot-

19

falls could be heard as they passed in the night. These were not the meanderings of an animal, but premeditated steps. An animal would surely have smelled the horses and come to investigate.

Just then the horse of John of Metz stomped one of his great hooves to throw off a biting insect. Fear became panic. Now they would be attacked in the darkness, perhaps never seeing the faces of their enemy.

Then, as suddenly as the horse had stomped, the mysterious visitors turned into one man and a horse. The stranger, realizing he was not alone in the woods, mounted the horse he had been leading, and fled.

"It was one man leading his horse."

"Yes. We are so jumpy I imagined a group of cutthroats ready to rob us of our teeth and kill us for sport."

Tension broke with the admission of their rootless terror.

"We will not be harmed," Joan said calmly. "I am on a military errand for God, and shall be protected all the way."

Her protectors might have been more convinced of her military errand had she not asked such naive questions about the army. After all, most generals who expected to save a nation had at least ridden horseback into battle at one time, and that was more than this general had done. Yet they agreed that she was a good rider by instinct, and they told her so.

There were probably more than a few winks passing

among her escort as they listened to her talk of victory without a battle plan. They even suspected that Captain Baudricourt had wrung his hands over what to do with this girl before packing her off, via the Burgundy woods, to the Dauphin's advisors. They decided by common consent that the captain was merely washing his hands of a touchy situation. All they knew for sure, in February, 1429, was that Bertrand of Poulengy, John of Metz, d'Aulon, and several archers were commissioned to travel by night, sleep by day, and deliver a seventeen-year-old girl to the Dauphin. The route through Burgundy was within French borders, but the people's sympathies were cold toward France and lukewarm toward the English. The land was ruled by Duke Philip, who was to pit his life against Charles VII and Joan the Maid.

For Joan there were two significant stops along the route. One was at the Abbey of Saint Urbain, where she heard mass, and the other at the Shrine of Saint Catherine at Fierbois. In both places she must have heard the voices, because her sense of responsibility to save France was greatly heightened, and her enthusiasm for the mission became contagious to her protectors. From here on, instead of questions about her battle plan, they quizzed her about victory.

Days passed, and finally the high stone walls of Chinon castle, punctuated by grey, austere towers, came into Joan's vision. This was the home of the Dauphin, son of Charles VI and Isabella of Bavaria. The twenty-six-year-

21

old prince was somewhere inside the castle walls, doubting that he would ever succeed his father as king of France. At the age of seven he was the intended king, but wars and rumors of illegitimacy had kept him uncrowned.

The Dauphin had a dual personality. He ran hot and cold on every issue, depending upon who was persuading him. He was a puppet on a string, tossed about by the great political and military currents of the fifteenth century. He was fainthearted, weak, and easily swayed, but sincere in his intention to do what was right. When most people called him feeble, Joan called him gentle.

It was a moment of truth for Joan as she entered the great hall at Chinon. Through months of delay she had waited for this very moment. Curious onlookers stood on cold stone walls beneath the great arches. The moment was more awesome than her entry to see the captain at Vaucouleurs. The people stared, tittered, gawked, and smiled.

"Is this the maid who will save France?" "She is only a child!"

"Hail the general," someone mocked.

But Joan's eyes were intent only upon the throne, and as she approached it she was aware that something was wrong. The young man seated there was obviously not the Dauphin. She turned from side to side, searching the faces, and finally, behind several people, she picked out the Dauphin himself.

"My lord, I would know you anywhere." Kneeling, she added, "The way has been made clear for me to save France and crown you king. For this deed I was born."

In astonishment the people pressed closer, but the Dauphin extended his hand and led her into his private chapel.

No one will ever know for sure what questions were asked and what answers were given in the chapel that day between the intended king of France and the girl who had come to crown him. Maybe she offered him proof of her errand for God. Maybe she told him of her voices. Perhaps she proved to him that he was legitimately of the House of Valois. Whatever happened, Joan instilled confidence in the young man and set him toward their common goal. Yes, he was to be king of France. Yes, he was of royal blood. Yes, his army could drive England from Orléans and from French soil.

But, as the Dauphin was swayed by Joan, he was easily swayed back again by his general, the Duke de la Tremoille. The general argued that this maid was an overenthusiastic peasant who had heard too many rumors about courageous martyrs for great causes. Although the Dauphin wanted Joan to be successful, he did not want to carry the blame if she failed. He was always on the brink of washing his hands of the affair and running off.

The Duke de la Tremoille, who was the Dauphin's confidant, was as untrustworthy as he was scheming. A traitor to the cause of France, he was crafty and rude, with an interest in three camps—French, English, and Burgundian. While advising Charles, he was selling arms to the English from his home at Sully and keeping secret correspondence with Philip of Burgundy. When the Dauphin wavered, Tremoille gave him decisions; when he swayed, Tremoille gave him unsound security.

Charles housed Joan in the Tower of Coudray. It looked so much like a prison that Joan must have questioned the prince's intentions, until he assigned a page to serve her. Louis de Contes was to serve her not only in the tower but on the battlefield. He believed in her voices, her mission, and her ability. Such loyalty must have meant a great deal to Joan, for friends were hard to come by.

Charles, in order to strengthen his belief in Joan's sanity, put two conditions upon his agreement to allow her to ride to Orléans. She must prove the truth of her conviction, and she must prove that she was a virgin. If either condition proved false, he would not give his consent to her mission.

In April, Joan was sent to the Council of Poitiers, made up of church officials and University of Paris professors.

"You are presuming to speak for God," they insisted, "and this is heresy in the name of the church."

"I do speak for God," she said. "I am His messenger on an errand to crown the king and save my country."

"Show us a miracle if you are from God. Surely you can do this to prove your authority."

"I am not a miracle worker. I do not pretend to work miracles. God will work the miracle through me if I am allowed to go to Orléans. Send me freely to Orléans, and this will be the sign of victory you require."

Heads shook, fingers pointed, tongues wagged, and eyes squinted, but still the inquisition at Poitiers wore on.

"I cannot raise the dead, cure disease, or straighten the crippled. God has need of me and I must be about my appointed task to crown the king. Please let me go freely."

And so it was that in April, 1429, the Council at Poitiers let her go and cleared her character and intention. They may not have believed her, but underneath the relentless questioning they were nagged by the unanswerable: "What if she really is from God?"

The second test was every bit as important for Joan as the first, but she knew as she rode to Tours that the fact of her virginity would prove that she was telling the truth. At Tours she was sent to Queen Yolande and her matrons, who accepted the fact that Joan was a maid. They cleared her character just as the Council had cleared her conviction.

After this second test, enthusiasm grew for her legitimate heavenly errand. Those who had referred to her as the peasant girl now called her Joan. Those who had followed her as a maid who heard voices now unhesitatingly saw her as *the* maid who heard voices and could save France. They rallied without being rallied. They supported her by choice rather than by force.

The Duke of Alençon gave Joan a beautiful horse on which she would ride into battle. The Dauphin gave her a suit of armor. A Scotsman living in Tours made her a flag to carry. She was also offered a sword, but she turned it down, saying, "The sword I must carry will be found behind the shrine of Saint Catherine at Fierbois."

A soldier was quickly sent to bring the sword, "if there be one." And (either in legend or in fact) a sword was brought from behind the shrine, just as Joan's voices had directed.

As the soldier entered the room with the sword, Louis de Contes, John of Metz, Bertrand of Poulengy, Jean Pasquerel (Joan's priest and confessor), and the Dauphin shook their heads in wonder. Only Joan was unmoved. This was another sign that she was being led by sources beyond their understanding.

In mid-April the Dauphin moved his court to Blois. His mind was on a perpetual seesaw as to whether Orléans could be saved. He knew that the city, in English hands for six months, was the key to everything south of the Loire River. Military success at Orléans was a crossroad to his coronation.

At Blois, Joan saw her troops for the first time, and she was appalled. These were not soldiers. They were drunkards, lazy peasants, forced prisoners, and, worst of all, a large group of women who followed the army.

"Have I just come thirty miles from Tours for this?" Joan asked. "Is this the army who will sound the battle cry through Orléans and allow God to be victorious?"

Joan's leadership was never more strongly asserted or heeded than it was at Blois, where the troops assembled before the battle for Orléans. She told them that victory was possible. The English could be driven out of France. The Dauphin could be king. France could be great again. The men listened and responded. They sat up and then stood up. Joan believed in them and told them so. She built up their courage step by step, and by nightfall these rascals and ruffians were straightening their backbones.

"The women must go home," she told Jean Pasquerel, the priest.

"But we cannot force them to go," he answered. "What shall we say to them?"

"Say that these men are on an errand for the salvation of France and the women must leave! If they will not go freely, we must drive them from camp."

The women did not go. They called Joan names, such as witch, sorceress, and harlot, but she was unmoved. She knew that her calling was not to answer the women but to persistently instil courage in her troops. At dusk Joan whisked the last woman out of camp, by determination and the flat side of her sword.

That night Joan announced that each man must do two things before starting for Orléans. By midnight each must confess his sins before God, and at dawn each must receive the Holy Sacrament on bended knee, to pay homage to the King of Heaven, who would, through them, bring peace to France.

It is likely that a great outcry followed her announcement, but, nevertheless, the priests passed among the men hearing confessions. At dawn all knelt in silence, receiving the Holy Sacrament.

Then Joan mounted her horse, holding in her hand the flag that the Scotsman had made. On one side of the silk was Christ being attended by two angels, the lily of France beside them. On the other side was the Virgin Mary looking at the French shield, which bore a gold fleur-de-lis.

Two pennants were also mounted on the pole which Joan held so proudly. One showed the annunciation (an angel telling Mary she was to be the mother of Jesus). The other was Joan's personal pennant—a white dove on a blue field.

Without fanfare, the battalion started out.

Orléans was thirty miles across the Loire River. Joan the Maid led archers, knights, squires, soldiers carrying ammunition, and wagons carrying food for besieged Orléans. She headed toward the great gate, for there was no thought in her mind of sneaking in the back door. She was proud of her army and confident of its success. She knew that God had not brought her all the way from a Domrémy pasture to trick her.

Flanked by the Duke of Alençon and other close friends, she glanced over her shoulder at the train of supporters, and called their attention to the unfurled flag and pennants.

Among the soldiers were two of Joan's brothers, who

had brought messages from home. They also brought with them a ring from her mother and father, which was inscribed with the names Jesus and Mary. Joan's parents had slowly accepted her errand, and they expected her to return to Domrémy when the deed was done.

The seventeen-year-old girl called out to her troops, "The way is clear before me. For this deed I was born."

Joan of Arc's mission for God at Orléans was becoming a reality.

CHAPTER FOUR

SAINTLY STRATEGY

❧❧❧❧ THE young girl rode back and forth, watching over her spiritually scrubbed troops. Her confident air gave the men courage, but the generals knew that she did not have the faintest idea of a battle plan.

Although Orléans was just thirty miles away, in the spring rain it seemed longer.

"How shall we cross the swollen Loire, Maid?"

"There will be a way, sir."

"I have heard that English soldiers circle the city three-deep, and hover over great battle machines which mow their enemies like a scythe."

"What you have heard sounds like it came from an English soldier, my friend."

From time to time she heard expressions of doubt as she passed among the soldiers and they aired their fears. But the great current was with her, and she felt it swell in the way the men marched and broke into song now and then. Her cry, "For God and for France," stirred

31

the most apathetic soldier. It was the basic motivation that whipped verve into the dullest among them.

Joan's troops were proud of her. Their respect was tested again and again as they talked to each other without swearing and went obediently to confession and mass as Joan required. They were now part of her holy cause "for God and for France," as on April 27, 1429, three thousand marched from Blois toward Orléans.

Orléans was a city of fifteen thousand people situated on the Loire River at the point closest to Paris. It had been part of several disputes between the French and English, and the battles had begun when the treaties had failed.

After England took Orléans, victorious troops stayed on as an army of occupation. It was their pattern to do this. The English could not always conquer the entire population, but they would take the gates to the city, raise battle cries for several days, unfurl the Union Jack, and declare themselves conquering heroes.

The native population, in turn, would be left without a supply route for food. Starvation and disease would creep in, monotony would set them at each other's throat, and plundering by English soldiers would keep them on constant alert. From time to time the soldiers walking in the streets would be dropped by a stray arrow from the French underground, which worked incessantly. Sometimes food supplies mysteriously came through the gates at night while English soldiers celebrated some national holiday or when the weather was so foul that it drove the guards from the watchtowers.

In December, 1428, an English general named John Talbot had arrived with two thousand men and had built stronger fortifications around the city. A thirty-foot stone wall with twenty-four towers was erected. Two towers on the south side faced the Loire, and drawbridges connected the towers to two stone-walled piers that protected the archers as they shot arrows at the enemy.

These fortifications looked awesome to the Orléans citizens, and the towers seemed to shout insults at the tower of Notre Dame de Cléry, the largest church in Orléans.

Rumors of Joan the Maid had swept away the aura of hopelessness in Orléans. At first the people had prayed for a French leader to rally the country, but none had come. Then they prayed for their own schemes to subdue their English aggressors. Now rumors flew that a seventeen-year-old girl was their guide to freedom. Stories grew and grew about her power, and some actually thought of her as having wings fluttering in a halo of light.

"You must enter the city tonight," the French General La Hire said to Joan. "The people need to see that you are not a ghost but a flesh-and-blood person. They need your courage to chase away the memories of the past six months. I shall lead you into Orléans after dark."

Joan agreed to the plan, and hastily called for two men who could read and write to take down a message for

33

General Talbot. "I appeal to you once again to withdraw your English troops from Orléans," the message read. "Such action will save your necks and your souls."

Joan rolled up the letter after they had read it to her several times, and handed it to Guienne, a military aide.

"Do not be afraid, Guienne," she said. "Ambleville will go with you, and by the rules of war you cannot be harmed as a messenger."

Hours dragged by as they waited for Talbot's response. Finally, Ambleville returned alone, and breathlessly explained that Guienne was being held prisoner. He repeated, with lowered eyes, the words "witch," "harlot," and "sorceress," which the English had called Joan. But Joan made no response, knowing that the enemy had sealed its own fate.

In the dark of night, La Hire came to Joan and cautiously rowed her across the Loire. The guards could be heard but not seen in the darkness as the redeemer of Orléans entered the city.

People crowded by torchlight to greet her. Some tried to touch her. Others brought their sick for healing. She spoke to them in small groups, giving them courage and hope, but insisted that she was only a mortal. They took her as she was and still hoped. If generals would be as easy to persuade as the citizens of Orléans, Joan felt, she would not lose so much strength through arguing. It was true that the French generals were always on the fence as to whether to let this young peasant lead their troops. In their minds, she was more useful as a mascot.

A turning point came for the military with a much-needed wind change that would enhance the safety of barges coming up the river. At almost the same time that the French were discussing their plight, the wind changed from east to west, and their thinking changed favorably, too.

In Orléans, Joan was led to the home of Jacques Boucher, treasurer to the Duke of Orléans. It was here that she prayed, fasted, and prepared for battle. Historians have suggested that her host may have been the only person to see her conversing with the voices.

It was only a matter of hours before the English knew that the Maid had arrived in the city. The very air felt different. Orléans seemed not so much like a city under siege, but like a city of victors. Bells rang in several churches; there were lively groups in the streets; and singing could be heard. English rumor said that Sir John Fastolf was leading an English battalion toward Orléans from Paris. They knew of his victory at Rouvray in 1429, and hopes ran high that he would arrive before the Maid sounded the attack.

Medieval battles were rather orderly, and for the most part the rules were obeyed by both sides. They fought by day and rested and cared for their wounded by night. They never fought on holy days, and enemies had even been known to celebrate Christmas together. Messengers, flag-bearers, and clergy went unarmed and were not molested by enemy soldiers.

In the early morning, through a deep sleep, Joan's

voices told her that French blood was being spilled. She stood fully awake, calling for someone to help her don her battle dress and ready her horse. At this moment she knew that her generals had out-schemed her, and she rode with fury.

"Courage," she shouted, riding into the midst of the battle at Saint Loup outpost. "For God and for France!"

She watched generals Jean Dunois and La Hire riding ferociously, thrusting their lances into the enemy. The sight of blood and suffering was sickening to her, although she knew it to be the way of war. So great was her sense of being on an errand for God that not all the dying cries of English soldiers could turn her away. It is said that she helped one English soldier by praying beside him as he lay in the last moments of agony.

"We have prisoners," yelled Dunois, galloping across the field. "Some crafty English tried to escape by dressing as priests. They are not afraid of being prisoners, but they are afraid of you, Maid. If you have God on your side, they are afraid to fight. Others believe you are a witch and they are afraid."

"Whatever they thought," Joan replied, "we have won the battle at Saint Loup for my heavenly King, and France is on the way to freedom."

The French troops were jubilant, and courage swelled in their hearts. This first taste of victory drove them eagerly toward another battle. Now they were more sure of themselves, and they were completely sure of Joan's powers.

"We won and shall win once more. Hail, soldiers! Let us make ready to fight again," an archer shouted.

"Every tower shall be laid low and every Englishman driven to the sea," yelled another.

Joan knew that it was not necessary to take every one of the twenty-four towers, but only to conquer enough so that the enemy would withdraw by its own volition, and French flags would again fly from the city gates.

Their eagerness for battle was cut off by Joan as she reminded her soldiers that there would be no fighting the next day because it was the Feast of the Ascencion. Her men were to go to confession again and to hear Mass at dawn. At this moment they would have followed her across Europe, so going to confession seemed like a small order.

"We must bind up our wounded and help bury the dead," Joan told them.

At last she returned to the Boucher home and fell on her knees, thanking God for guidance and victory. The day never came when Joan failed to show humility. She knew she was a servant on an errand, and the victory belonged to God. She was only carrying out orders.

Madame Boucher urged her to eat and sleep to gain strength for another battle, but Joan prayed on and on. Her power of concentration in prayer was so great that she did not see Madame Boucher or know that Dunois and La Hire had come to make plans for further military encounters. Often they held meetings and even skirmishes without her, but when she heard their plans she invariably proposed different ones. At the last minute it was always Joan's plans that were used. She moved supply barges, ordered ammunition, arranged troops, and kept up their courage. Leadership was a natural gift to Joan, and common sense was her greatest blessing, besides the voices.

The Maid wanted to storm the Tourelles. These two towers with their drawbridges were the strongest English fortifications, guarded by six hundred men. Archers and gunners crawled over the entire area, awaiting the attack.

To Pasquerel, her friend and priest, she said, "Stay by me all day, for I have much to do. Besides, I have been told that tomorrow I will be wounded and blood will flow from above my heart."

This statement gave Pasquerel a sinking feeling. He was afraid that they would lose Joan in battle, and even though his belief in the voices had been sincere, he wavered briefly and closed his eyes in horror. Earlier Joan had stepped on a spike in the field at Saint Augustin outpost, and he had feared that infection would set in. A wound above the heart!

"I shall not die," she told him. "Do not be afraid. My errand for God is not over because the Dauphin cannot be crowned at Rheims until the English are gone, and I shall live to see the mission through. Leave me now. I must prepare for battle."

Pasquerel left, knowing that her preparation meant prayer, not the sharpening of her sword.

"Run, you soldier of a witch. We are ready for battle.

Where is your little angel, eh?" The French soldiers heard these taunts as they prepared to take the Tourelles.

The next few hours were filled with fierce battle. Some of the English were determined to wear down these men who followed the directions of a girl, but others fought with deep reservations as to whether they were fighting God's own plan. Some even threw down their weapons and ran into the woods. Others gladly became prisoners.

Joan's flag seemed to be everywhere at once, so quickly did she cover the fighting territory. The winds kept her flags unfurled, and they waved as though they were being held for every soldier on both sides to see.

The English battle machines were unwieldy, and hand-fighting quickly took their place. The short-handled battle-axes left many men mutilated on the field. Arrows flew from the unseen archers at the stone piers which jutted from one end of the drawbridge over the Loire River. Maces were flung, and long-handled lances plucked men from their horses and left them dying.

"Courage—take courage—for God and for France!" Joan's cry was taken up by the men, and it was heard everywhere as they fought and as they died.

Suddenly, as if from nowhere, an arrow pierced Joan above her heart. She was bleeding badly and she twisted in pain. Pasquerel immediately saw what had happened, and he caught her as she slid from her horse. He laid her tenderly on the ground, and then several soldiers carried her from the field into the woods.

"She is bleeding hard. What shall we do?"

39

"Go and fetch the woman who sings magic to stop blood from flowing."

"That is superstition," Joan cried. "Stay here. The blood will stop soon and I shall go back with my army." With that, Joan pulled out the arrow.

Suddenly La Hire appeared with a broken messsage of "men afraid you are dead . . . can only retreat."

With great vigor Joan stood up, and the blood stopped flowing. The men moved back, feeling that they had witnessed a miracle. Joan mounted her horse and rode slowly toward the Tourelles.

At their first sight of her, the French soldiers began to fight with renewed strength. They scaled walls on the first try. They picked up Englishmen bodily and threw them into the muddy river.

Retreat had never been in Joan's thinking, and as she watched her flag touch the wall as a signal to fight harder, she knew that victory belonged to God.

She continued to give mercy and pity where it was needed. Her sense of suffering and sorrow was intense, and men crying in pain never failed to overwhelm her with emotion. As she knelt among them she saw a great barge on the river burst into flames, and saw men making their way above the flames on what seemed to be long strips of metal to replace the broken drawbridge. They were Frenchmen taking the tower.

"Here is Glasdale, Maid!" came shouts from the tower. "Here is the enemy dying for his cause!"

Suddenly Joan saw the English general Glasdale of the Tourelles being consumed in the flames from the barge passing beneath the makeshift drawbridge on which he was being held prisoner. Shouts of victory were heard even as the general fell into the Loire.

"It is done. God's victory is reality," Joan whispered to herself.

The last cries of the dying were smothered in shouts of victory. Joan fell to her knees, giving thanks for those who had given their lives and those who had brought about victory for God and for France.

Dunois of Orléans jumped from his horse, interrupting her prayer, and exclaimed his joy over the battle. With him was Guienne, Joan's freed messenger.

From that day on, Joan was known as the Maid of Orléans. All night people celebrated their victory, but Joan, in her room at Jacques Boucher's home, was giving thanks and concentrating on the Dauphin's coronation.

41

✠ CHAPTER FIVE ✠

DETOUR TO A CORONATION

❋❋❋ WHEN Joan rode toward Tours and the Dauphin after the victorious battle of Orléans, she wore the dream of his coronation on her sleeve. Everyone could feel it. The peak of her errand for God was the coronation of the rightful king of France.

"My lord, my king. The battle is over and Orléans is French again. Let us go to Rheims." She knelt before him with expectation bubbling from her soul.

"But the victory was a solitary one, Maid," he answered. "It does not mean the enemy has turned and run home. We cannot go to Rheims yet."

A war of wills was on. Charles remained unsure about his coronation. Between Orléans and Rheims lay council meeting after council meeting and scheme after scheme. La Tremoille kept Charles cautious, and Joan kept him on the edge of eagerness. It was a time of waiting, debating, and hesitation.

This constant indecision watered down Joan's happiness. Her close friends, d'Aulon, Louis de Contes, and Pasquerel, shook their heads and held their tongues. They felt that they had been tricked, and they wondered whether Joan had. They also wondered what other detours on the road to Rheims would have to be made.

"We must take all the English forts on the Loire before the coronation," Charles declared.

"All the English . . ." and Joan's voice melted with disbelief. Her eyes closed and her shoulders dropped, as if physical exhaustion had suddenly overtaken her.

"You must return to Orléans and reprovision the army," the Dauphin continued. "There will be no coronation before the English footprints are wiped from the Loire valley."

Without argument, Joan mounted her horse.

"We go to Orléans to reprovision our forces." She did not look at her accompanying escort, but she knew they followed.

"Charles is running hot and cold again," the men said. "He is weak!"

Joan heard their bitter grumblings, but she only rode a little faster and said nothing. If ever she needed encouragement from her voices it was now, but they did not speak. She reviewed her instructions to crown the king, and she wondered whether or not she had misinterpreted the directives. The hours passed, and she decided that the coronation would ultimately happen, and perhaps her eagerness had run away with her good sense.

44

Orléans was ecstatic with joy at having Joan back. The citizens believed in her power, rejoiced in her ability, and adored her as their special Maid of Orléans. Her wish was their command, and army provisions began to roll from bursting carts.

Joan avoided her worshippers and ignored the holy atmosphere that was building around her. People trailed her for physical healings, although she kept insisting that she was mending a nation, not broken bodies. Her humility made them believe in her more than ever. Often she was asked to hold babies for baptism, which she did, naming the girls "Joan" and the boys "Charles."

"To arms!" Joan shouted to her faithful soldiers, and they mustered so professionally that they looked like they could conquer the world. Men came from miles around to join the victors. They would follow Joan's banner wherever it led, make their confessions, hear Mass, and rustle up enthusiasm for any campaign.

It was lucky for Joan that Fastolf, the English general, was as cautious and undecisive as La Tremoille. Fastolf kept the English troops cautious; La Tremoille kept the Dauphin cautious. Neither was deaf to the rumblings of the English soldiers that Joan was bewitched and that they would rather turn tail than fight her powers. In the wake of such utter defeat at Orléans, the waves of fear grew stronger.

When the Loire campaign started, Joan sensed dissension in the ranks. Some of her men were eager to attack Jargeau and they pressed her for action. Others feared the arrival of Fastolf and thought that the entire Loire campaign should be abandoned. But Joan planned to attack.

Jargeau was held by General Suffolk and English soldiers who had retreated from Orléans. They guarded their garrison amid the rumors that Joan's white banner had been seen and that an attack by thousands of French soldiers was imminent. Some of the English crept away into the night in fear of this "witch."

Joan planned to attack at dawn, but some of her men became overzealous and hit the outskirts of the town that night. The English, in turn, held their ground. Joan changed plans, swung her banner into the air, and shouted, "To arms, to arms! At them bravely!"

During the skirmish, a messenger arrived from Suffolk asking for a fifteen-day truce, but it did not take Joan long to figure out that he was only stalling to wait for Fastolf's five thousand troops. She said, "No!"

Ladders were thrown over the walls into Jargeau, and Joan, while scaling a wall, was hit on the head with a stone and knocked down. Her recovery was quick, however, and with fighting all around, she shouted to Alençon that he was in great danger and should move. Within minutes, the spot where he had stood was blown up by a cannonball.

Suffolk was taken prisoner, twelve hundred Englishmen lay dead, five hundred became prisoners, and Jargeau became French.

Three days later an attack was made at Meung, four hours' journey from Orléans. This was another site held by soldiers who had retreated from Orléans. Their general was Talbot. The English gave only light resistance, and Talbot fled to Patay.

French troops camped at Beaugency, five miles from Meung. While they were filling their stomachs with food and their souls with Joan's required masses, French scouts arrived with the news that a great army was approaching. Surely this was Fastolf, upon whom lay all the English hopes.

Suddenly, as from nowhere, a dark charger raced toward Joan. She could see that the rider was French and not English.

"It is Arthur de Richemont of Brittany, the constable of France," Joan said.

Joan knew that de Richemont, an archenemy of La Tremoille, had talked Charles into giving him an army to hold back English pressures. She knew, too, that he was a valiant soldier.

"I have come with two thousand men to fight with you until the English are driven home," de Richemont told her.

"Your coming was not my desire, but you are welcome."

"If he stays, I go," said the Duke of Alençon, Joan's own military leader.

"We must work together," Joan said calmly. With that, de Richemont took his place beside Joan, while the

47

duke hid his jealousy. De Richemont's men fell into position, swelling the ranks.

In the meantime, the woods near Patay were crawling with English soldiers who waited hour after hour for the sight of a Frenchman. Five hundred archers squatted behind the bushes in a wooded area known as La Beauce, while the bulk waited on a plateau.

Before the arrival of de Richemont, Joan had sent seventy knights as an advance guard to spy on the enemy.

"You may be assured," she told them, "that the English shall be beaten. Even if they take refuge in the clouds, we shall have them."

As the knights moved through La Beauce, a frightened deer darted from the woods. A cry was heard; the enemy had been located! With great haste a guard rode to inform the French army, but before the entire army returned, every English archer had been killed and Fastolf had taken the rest of his men toward Paris. He refused to fight the Maid when victory, whether by witchery or with the help of God, was raining down upon her.

Talbot was taken prisoner, and the Loire campaign ended.

After these victories, most generals would have marched to free Paris from the enemy, but Joan had not received heavenly orders to take the city. She was going to Rheims.

Her enthusiasm was contagious, and even the Dauphin almost caught it. Except for the inner circle in the court, everyone believed in her errand for God. Her army swelled, and her reputation of holiness grew. The campaign toward Rheims could bring nothing but success; had she not said this from the day she left Domrémy?

On or about July 1, the French army numbered between ten thousand and twelve thousand men, but the previous campaigns had taken them farther and farther from their Orléans base. Provisions, food, and funds were running low. At Auxerre, in order to avoid a battle, the English people handed over a few provisions to the troops and two thousand crowns as a bribe to La Tremoille, who had joined the march to Rheims, to insure that their town would be left in peace. Joan was furious that La Tremoille had allowed the English to bribe him, but she yielded on the basis that no lives would be lost.

Charles had also joined the troops, and he was as indecisive as ever as he waited for Auxerre to agree to unconditional surrender.

Three days later, Troyes followed suit, and not only negotiated for compromises but fed the army on beans which months before had been planted in response to a visionary preacher, Brother Richard. To the hungry troops, even this seemed a part of Joan's heavenly authority.

The peace negotiations at Troyes took several days, but Joan kept assuring Charles that he would be master of that city as well as Rheims in just a few days.

The English tried to keep the French prisoners whom they had found on the fringes of the army and captured, but Joan was indignant and demanded that Charles pay one silver piece per head to ransom them.

Joan moved her troops to Châlons, which also surrendered. From there, Charles and Joan each wrote a letter to the Duke of Burgundy in Rheims, asking him to surrender and warning that he could not hope to oppose the swelling French army.

The duke could not make up his mind. If he surrendered, his army would be furious at his cowardice. If he failed to surrender, the people of Rheims would rise against him, so great was their fear of Joan's power. A battle meant the preparation of munitions, troops, and the walls themselves. Finally, the string of French victories, as well as the rumors concerning the number of French troops, shook his confidence. The Duke surrendered.

On July 16, Charles, Joan, and all the troops entered the city of Rheims. The loyal French citizens who had been under siege were jubilant, and Joan breathed deeply as she anticipated the completion of her errand.

The coronation of Charles VII was set for the next day, July 17, 1429, a Sunday.

In Domrémy, Joan's voices had hummed in her mind, and she had once felt that they were tricks of her imagination. Later she felt that they would forget her one day. No one knows what made her realize that the voices were to be obeyed, but as Joan did obey, the voices guided her on and on. It took just five months to go from Domrémy to Rheims—a miracle in itself, considering the barriers a seventeen-year-old girl of any time would face in pleading for an army and preparing to crown a king.

Overcoming every barrier, Joan and all the king's men had pieced together the French kingdom.

Rheims held its breath as royalty and peasantry alike streamed into the city. Everyone was wide-eyed with anticipation.

The site of the coronation was to be the Rheims cathedral, which was nearing completion after two hundred years. Medieval craftsmen had molded it into breathtaking magnificence. It was the official coronation site for French kings. The archbishop of Rheims, Regnault de Chartres, had not been in the cathedral for over twenty years because of the occupation of the city by the English.

The coronation took place with all due ceremony, even though it was a time of war. The crown was in English hands; the holy anointing oil was hidden; the banners were wrapped and closeted; the sword and scepter were held by the English at Saint-Denis; and celebrations were almost out of style because the wars had lasted so long.

All night people gathered in Rheims, and those who were not helping to unfurl banners were beginning to celebrate the coronation of Charles VII.

The marshals of France rode all the way to the Abbey of Saint-Denis so that the king could be anointed with holy oil from the phial which had been mysteriously filled for each coronation since the time of Saint Clovis.

51

At nine o'clock in the morning, Charles VII began his long processional down the main aisle of the great church. Close to the front pew he unknowingly passed Jacques d'Arc, father of the Maid of Orléans, who had come to be near his daughter on this day. Neither Jacques nor Charles could scarcely believe that all this was really taking place, and each man in his own way wore a look of unreality. Neither knew that the other, too, had held reservations about Joan.

The Maid of Orléans, dressed in full armor and holding her banner, knelt beside the altar as Charles approached. She rose as he came near, and perhaps said to herself once again, "To this deed I was born." Never had she felt that she was more than an instrument in God's hands for this occasion. The glory and victory were God's glory and victory. She remained an errand girl.

The names of twelve peers were read, and Joan listened as the dukes of Burgundy, Aquitaine, and Normandy were called enemies of the king. Three ecclesiastics were present: the archbishops of Rheims, Laon, and Châlons. Some, like the bishop of Beauvais, were absent because they were English sympathizers.

The people pressed hard against each other to see the king as he took his oath to protect France and to rule with justice. Then, with great pomp, the Archbishop of Rheims lifted the borrowed crown and placed it on the head of Charles VII, saying "Noel."

Joan knelt before the king, and with tears in her eyes,

said, "Now has God's will been fulfilled. You are the true king to whom all France belongs."

The ceremony, which lasted five hours, came to a close as "Noel" resounded throughout the cathedral and out into the streets.

Joan went to her father, and with great emotion, they held each other, each asking forgiveness of the other and each offering it.

In a few days Jacques started for home, expecting Joan to follow close behind. He had been given a horse by the king himself, and, at the request of Joan, a tax exemption for Domrémy, which was repealed many years later.

Joan stood in her spotlight in history at this moment. Her voices had brought her all the way from her father's pasture to the altar of Rheims cathedral. If she had expected great ovations from Charles, her disappointment did not show. It was reward enough to do God's will. The deed for which she was born had been fulfilled.

CHAPTER SIX

PRIZE CATCH

✠✠✠✠ THE coronation was over, but Joan still urged a march on Paris. As long as the English walked the streets, France could not be a unified country, and anyone could see that the time was ripe for running the English to the channel. Joan's idea was to march eighty miles to Paris. A surprise attack, riding on the crest of the coronation, would expel the enemy and free the captives. The two thousand soldiers guarding Paris could be taken easily by Joan's ten thousand men.

But while Joan burned for Paris, the king wavered. For four days he rode in and out of little towns, smiling, waving, and receiving loyalty gifts, from wine bottles to cows. Every time Paris was mentioned he swung back and forth on his string of indecision.

La Tremoille, now forty-four years old, was a man filled with schemes to protect himself. His connections in the English, Burgundian, and French camps kept him on the alert lest he betray his connection with one to the others.

La Tremoille's early fear was that Joan would win the king's favor. Later he was afraid that she would become queen of France by popular demand, but the ever-present rumors of witchery soon reduced this fear. His greatest worry was that France would become united, and he would lose the personal profits from those towns which bought his protection or his munitions.

For the next month King Charles and La Tremoille were caught in a flurry of delegations, conspiracies, rumors of treaties, and messengers to Philip of Burgundy. With one ear they listened to the generals planning an attack on Paris. With the other they listened to suggestions of concessions and secret treaties. There was to be a truce until Christmas in towns north of the Seine, which were ready to become French again. Charles could attack Paris, but not for fifteen days. This allowed England to take hold more securely in northern France, and also gave Philip time to refortify Paris.

During the truce, everyone was to be working for peace. Charles did nothing, but Philip was carefully planning.

Joan suspected a trick, and she pleaded with Charles that he was not in a position to make compromises. A successful battle was their only hope, but Charles refused to listen. She knew that the king was being manipulated by Philip of Burgundy and Bedford of England. Joan was not allowed to enter into the court activities. Charles lost out on every treaty, and when Joan was finally allowed to go to Paris it was already too late.

On September 8, 1429, Joan decided to strike. Since

this was a holy day for the Virgin Mary, she was reluctant to fight, but this was the day for battle and she had waited so long. She had many troops, but they were disorganized, and every military plan failed. Joan was wounded in the leg; her standard-bearer was killed.

"I shall not leave here until we take Paris!" she cried. But her words were lost as La Tremoille ordered a retreat to Saint-Denis, and Joan's military spark died.

A general's retreat is a symbol of defeat. It spreads gloom over the troops, and waves of exhaustion set in. The buoyancy is gone; verve and vigor die. Many of Joan's volunteers dropped out and went home. Some renewed their suspicions that her voices had deserted her, or that perhaps she was a witch after all.

Yet Joan would not take retreat as a final answer. She mustered a handful of faithful men to take the town of Saint Pierre le Moustier. No one in the court cared whether or not she risked her life, and no one interfered. If she won a town they would accept it for the king, but if she failed they would not rescue her.

After much difficulty, Joan did take Saint Pierre, and La Tremoille accepted it for the king with very little thanks.

In November, she attempted to take La Charité. Her army's provisions were so low that she begged the patriots of the city to send help if they wanted to be liberated. But they gave little aid, and after some weeks the cause was lost.

Winter came, and Joan was forced to stay in court.

She longed to be actively engaged in chasing the enemy, but instead she was kept on the fringes of political maneuvers and military strategy. The court moved to Sully, and she wandered unhappily through the bleak, grey halls of La Tremoille's castle. She stood at the high windows, feeling like a prisoner as she watched the wind blow the tree branches into weird patterns. It was a time for remembering warm, sunny days in the fields of Domrémy, and a time to project her hopes to the day that she would return there. It had been her plan to go back to Domrémy after Paris was taken.

One day a message arrived, and Joan hoped that it was good news. It came from the Catholics of Bohemia asking her to make a statement against the followers of church reformer John Huss, whom they labeled a heretic. Perhaps Joan had never heard of Huss, and if she had, her knowledge of his teachings and trial would have been sparse. But she did not hesitate to make the rigid statement that if his followers did not change their ways, she would take their lives with her sword.

Also during that bleak midwinter, Joan became unwisely involved with Jean d'Armagnac, who had written to ask her which of three popes should be obeyed. He added that if she did not know, she should ask Jesus Christ. Tossing humility aside, Joan said that she was too busy to find out the answer, but when she had more leisure time, she would take care of the matter.

At another time, when several women approached her

to touch their rosaries, Joan is reported to have said, "Touch them yourselves. Your touch is as good as mine."

Like the retreat of a wave from the shore, Joan's supporters began to fall away. King Charles ignored her; La Hire was given his own army; the Duke of Alençon was sent home; the voices were silent; French skirmishes were unsuccessful; and her sword was broken in two over the back of a woman who had been following the army.

From court gossip, she learned that the spring campaign would center at Compiègne, which had been loyal to France through every English-Burgundian pressure.

In April, 1430, Joan took off with a handful of men for Lagny. Then she changed her mind and headed for Melun. For several weeks she maneuvered back and forth, and it was obvious to her small force that she had no plan.

At Lagny, two events indicated the rising forces of pros and cons concerning Joan. First, Burgundian Captain Franquet was taken prisoner by the French. His guerrilla force had terrorized the area for some time. The Burgundians, furious that their captain should be subjected to prison, trial, and execution, held Joan responsible. Burgundian feelings rose against her.

The second event brought a great restoration in Joan's power. By custom, stillborn babies were laid upon the church altar, and young girls came to the chapel to pray them through limbo, which, according to the Catholic belief, is a purgatory for dead babies. Joan was asked, on one occasion, to join the girls in the chapel, and the child for whom they prayed began to breathe. The event was labeled a miracle, and Joan was lauded in a way that she had not been since Orléans, although she insisted that God had performed the miracle, not she.

English rumors of Joan's witchery again filled the air, and fears deepened that with such power she could take Paris with a wave of her hand.

Joan left Lagny for Melun, and, finally, after a long delay, her voices spoke.

"Joan, you will be captured before Saint John's Day. Do not be afraid. God will help you."

But Joan shook with fear. The voices had always brought hope, and now they pronounced doom. Joan was convinced that they meant she would die, and for the first time, she was afraid for herself. Numb with sadness, she asked many questions, but the voices kept repeating the same awesome message.

Never through the worst hours at Orléans had Joan known fear. Her courage had been displayed for every soldier to follow. But the rejection by Charles, the military disappointments, and the gathering gloom left her fearful for her life.

Joan remained in Melun for Easter of 1430, but she felt no joy of the season.

The truce that Charles had made with Duke Philip did not bring peace. Philip had withdrawn from the area, and rumors said that Paris was arming heavily. The months that Charles had merely stalled, while his enemies had continued to scheme against him, resulted in five more years of war and twenty more years of English occupation in France.

Joan had realized months before that England and Burgundy were trying to keep French forces divided by fighting simultaneously on several fronts—each front away from Paris. She warned Charles, but he turned a deaf ear.

Before any campaign, military strategists map the terrain and check nearby towns to see whether they are friend or foe. The towns of Beauvais, Crépy, Soissons, Choisy, and Margny were among those to be checked.

Beauvais was French, but it had an active English underground. When Charles tested its loyalty, the people opened the town gates with French songs and festivities. No one could doubt their sympathies as they presented him with gifts and ran the English sympathizers out of town. Among those who were exiled was the bishop of Beauvais, Pierre Cauchon, who would later become Joan's archenemy at her trial.

Charles knew that he had to hold the city of Compiègne in order to reach Paris. Joan's foresight forced her to rush to Compiègne.

Like Beauvais, Compiègne had been loyally French through every pressure. The citizens had liked Joan, and they had welcomed her after the battle of Orléans. But sometimes people have short memories, and Orléans was a year past. Just as Orléans had been the military key to

61

territory south of Paris, so Compiègne was now to the north of Paris.

In the meantime, La Tremoille had ignored the wishes of the Compiègne citizens that Guillaume de Flavy be made governor of their city. He took the job himself, and made Flavy his lieutenant.

Compiègne was surrounded by thick woods, and beyond the trees lay several smaller towns. Weeks passed with no major fighting. Everyone was on edge, knowing that sooner or later an attack would come and the fighting would be brutal and bloody. Joan's voices kept repeating their warning of capture. Finally, Joan was ordered to move a force of men against Margny in a sudden attack. The English-Burgundian forces were taken completely by surprise. In the midst of the fighting, Joan sent a messenger to Clairoix for more soldiers, and suddenly the bells of Compiègne started to ring. They were not the slow tolling after death or the happy peals of a Sabbath morning. They ran steadily, urgently, without pattern.

Suddenly, the woods were alive with enemies. It is said that Joan's five hundred men now faced six thousand. The French ran for their lives as they saw the crouched archers with their shining lances. They did not wait for the call of retreat, but streaked toward the protecting walls of Compiègne. Joan fought on; she would not consider retreat.

From a tower at Compiègne, Flavy watched the battle,

and saw Joan fighting from her charging horse. He saw the men scrambling for safety. When most of the men were safely inside he ordered the gate closed.

At last Joan rode for the gate, shouting, "Raise the barrier! Raise the barrier!" Time and again she shouted. The gate did not open. The enemy pressed down upon her and dragged her from her horse, demanding, "Surrender! Surrender!"

"I have already surrendered myself into God's keeping, and His authority is beyond yours," she said.

"Say surrender . . . say surrender!"

But Joan would not.

The English and Burgundians, however, were victorious without her saying the word.

Joan's faithful squire, d'Aulon, her brother Pierre, and a friend named Poton were also taken prisoner, but they were soon released.

Technically Joan was the prisoner of John of Luxembourg, since an archer from his land had captured her, but it was not long before far more eager hands grabbed for the prize.

English soldiers lined the approach to Margny to see this witch-general who had caused them so much trouble. Duke Philip himself came from Coudun to see her.

While the English celebrated, the loyal French were overwhelmed with sorrow. They prayed for her release, collected money for ransom, and readied themselves to kidnap her from English hands and hide her in safety. King Charles did nothing.

Many questions still remain unanswered concerning Joan's capture: Who ordered her to Margny that day? Who was responsible for her capture? Why was a rescue not attempted? Who ordered the chroniclers of the battle at Compiègne to ignore the entire event, erasing it for posterity?

The fact remains that Joan of Arc, at eighteen years of age, was taken prisoner on May 24, 1430, outside the closed gate of Compiègne, France.

For weeks John of Luxembourg dickered between the University of Paris, Duke Philip of Burgundy, and the English Duke of Bedford for the sale of his prize catch. The university finally cast its lot with the English, and would try Joan for the French Inquisition. Bedford wanted her death no matter who tried her, and Philip wanted her death to erase the aura of her as a living legend. John sold the Maid to England for sixteen thousand francs (then about three thousand dollars). Bishop Pierre Cauchon was the intermediary. Joan would be tried by the English and kept in an English prison, and if the trial did not convict her she was to be turned over to the English military. Everyone involved was intent upon Joan's death. Only the technique of execution had to be worked out.

CHAPTER SEVEN

TRIAL AND ERROR

✤✤✤✤ ". . . and the guard never sleeps."

"How could I escape in chains, sir?"

"Witches have ways, Maid."

"I do not know the ways of witches. I only know the way of my Guide."

"Can your guide break chains?"

"Not unless it is His will."

The guard snickered in the semidarkness of the stone dungeon.

It had been nearly a year since Joan had been taken prisoner and sold to the English. Now she stood on the brink of her fate. Charles had not sent a ransom; her friends had not attempted her rescue; and God was not performing a miracle for her.

February 21, 1431, dawned with the same monotony for Joan as it did for all those who were held in the Rouen prison.

Joan did not know that the verdict had been written

before her trial began. She was both wide-eyed with hope and chilled with terror. She had not watched the political maneuvering, the unethical choice of accusers, and the illegal traps laid by Cauchon.

Pierre Cauchon was a Frenchman who had English sympathies. He was a member of the Great Council of England. He was a personal friend of young Henry VI, the eight-year-old English king who had traveled as far as Calais, France, in April, 1430, to offset the publicity of Charles's coronation. Cauchon was a close friend of the Duke of Bedford's, and he had many associates at the University of Paris.

Now sixty years old, Cauchon knew that killing Joan without a trial might lead to a revolution because of her popularity with the people. To try her as an enemy of England would be no more than a state trial. To try her as a witch would mean that she could be burned, but no ransom would be offered. To have Joan dead, by whatever means, was his goal.

With scheming precision Cauchon served as the intermediary for payment to Luxembourg, and Joan was bound over to Cauchon for the ecclesiastical (church) trial. The charges stated that she had presumed to hear voices, see visions, and speak familiarly with God. Such presumption was heresy. She dressed as a boy, rallied soldiers to battle, and held secret talks with the French king. There were tales of the resurrection of a baby and the mystical discovery of a sword at Fierbois. Most important of all, she had achieved miraculous military victories and the coronation of a king. Cauchon was convinced that she could be nothing more than an ordinary witch, and hundreds of these were disposed of each year. This case differed only in that the prisoner had gained great popularity. By discrediting Joan's source of guidance, Cauchon could topple the authority of the coronation at Rheims.

There was no jury, but a handpicked board of sixty assessors were tagged for duty from their professional fields of medicine, law, and theology. Usually only six or eight assessors would hear a case.

Cauchon had no right to judge this case, since Joan was not from his ecclesiastical territory. Serving with him was a deputy of the Grand Inquisition of France.

Joan was not allowed counsel, nor was she housed in a prison tended by women.

The chapel of the Rouen archbishop's castle was heavy with solemnity. All those who had not seen the prisoner craned their necks over stiff robes toward the side door. Some scratched nervously in books, while others rubbed the wooden arms of their high-back chairs.

"Present the prisoner!"

Without flurry, a young priest, Isambard de la Pierre, led what looked like a young man through the arch. Still in boys' clothes, her hair cropped, Joan walked limply.

Amid the noise of clearing throats, Cauchon asked, "What is your name?"

"Joan d'Arc, sir."

"What is your father's name?"

"Jacques d'Arc of Domrémy, sir."

"Did you live in Domrémy with your father?"

"Yes, sir, and with my mother, Isabelle d'Arc."

"Tell us of those early years."

Joan told of her life, friends, and family.

"Why did you leave Domrémy?"

"Because voices told me that my Lord had need of me."

"And who is your lord?"

"The King of Heaven, sir."

One of the assessors asked, "What did the voices say, Joan?"

Joan quietly explained her communications with Saint Michael, Saint Margaret, and Saint Catherine, but refused to respond when her accusers asked about secret messages for Charles. She stalled them by saying such things as, "I shall tell you that two weeks from today."

At first her listeners accepted this, but the pressures grew. Hour after hour she stood while the others sat. Often she swayed in weakness, and her escort, Isambard, would prevent her from fainting.

At day's end questions were stopped because the assessors were tired, rather than because they had mercy for Joan.

For sixteen sessions she boldly supported her voices. They had advised bold speech and had promised God's

68

guidance. Never did she discredit Charles. She often acknowledged her failures, but never blamed her voices.

Again and again she refused to say the "Hail Mary" and "Our Father," trying to bargain with the accusers over permission to hear mass or have her confession heard.

As they continued to question her belief in visions and voices, Joan felt a breaking down among a few of the assessors. Some of them questioned her in kindness, and others were touched by her sincere convictions. In the end, only twenty-two assessors actually condemned her.

The lack of sleep and food, combined with fear and pressure, made Joan violently ill, and Cauchon, afraid that she might die of natural causes, had her treated.

Recognizing her illness as a good opportunity for private questioning, he adjourned court in the chapel and convened it with a handful of men in Joan's cell. Such a move was illegal, since she was entitled to full court hearings.

Joan must have felt very small and helpless as these robed men hovered over her in their relentless inquisition.

"Could you not remove the chains, sir?" she pleaded.

"You are our prisoner. The chains remain. Will you put on a dress, Maid?"

"When I am directed by my Lord to do so."

"I command you to put on a dress and take off boys' clothes."

"I cannot."

In exasperation, a dress was pushed through the bars and thrown at Joan's side as her visitors filed out of the cell.

No one knows whether or not Joan ever put on the dress, but a dress would not have changed the ultimate verdict at this mock trial.

On May 29, 1430, Joan was to hear her verdict. Inwardly, she knew that the words she heard would bring her death. She was loaded into a cart in the blazing sunlight. She had not seen the sun for weeks, and now it brought her only discomfort and near-blindness. She did not seem to be only nineteen, for her frail-looking body added many years. Her vigor was gone and her stamina was broken under the weight of this ordeal.

Joan's accusers kept close watch around the slowly moving cart. Her chains remained locked and they pulled at her with every jerk of the cart. The procession halted at the cemetery at the Abbey of Saint Ouen. Joan was led out of the cart by Father Ladvenu, a young priest who believed in her, but they were not allowed to speak together.

As was the custom, the prisoner had to hear a sermon before hearing her fate, and Guillaume Erard, canon of Rouen, preached in endless monotony.

Then, as coolly as ever, Pierre Cauchon read seventy articles of accusation against Joan, and a document of her excommunication.

"Do you recant of your sins? Do you beg for pardon? Where are your voices now? Where is your miracle? You will burn, Maid. You will burn in eternal flame."

"No, no—not burn! Do not burn me! Do not set me aflame!"

"Recant, recant!" Others echoed Cauchon's command, and Joan burst into tears of terror and fear. It seemed that everyone was against her. No one in all these months had come to her rescue.

"Mercy," she begged, "mercy!"

"Mercy will be shown you only if you sign your name to this confession."

And Joan, in panic and desolation, made a cross at the bottom of a little document of six or seven lines. Later Cauchon allowed the confession to be greatly lengthened.

Sobbing with defeat, Joan's bravery broke down, and no one who watched was unmoved. Her spirit was broken as completely as her body, and perhaps she was numb to the hands that guided her back into the cart and finally to the cell.

But Cauchon tasted victory lightly. Recantations were not enough—he wanted Joan's life. To simplify the proceedings, seventy accusations were whittled to twelve, any one of which meant prison, and a combination of which meant the stake. Her last words to Cauchon were, "Bishop, I die through you."

Burning Joan as a witch would not only break her pub-

71

lic image but would deaden the impact of King Charles. However, what Cauchon could not kill was the gathering force of her popularity with the people, and she remained their heroine.

The verdict was read again to Joan in her cell. Endlessly she had prayed that because of her recantation in the Saint Ouen cemetery, she would be pardoned. After her tears were gone she entered into so great a calm that it seemed as if she had received the help from God that had been promised by the voices. Quietly she donned the long gown customarily worn by the accused, and she gave thanks as a guard slipped the chains from her ankles.

Joan entered history as her life ended in the roaring flames. On May 30, 1431, she entered the company of mankind's immortals at the same time that King Charles, at Chinon, was writing "thank-you" letters to those who had helped him beyond the call of duty.

Her ashes were sacked and thrown into the Seine River, either to avoid the use of them as charms or to prevent her followers from establishing a holy site at her burial place.

CHAPTER EIGHT

CORRECTING THE ERROR

❧❧❧❧ TWENTY years after Joan's death, King Charles startled his advisors by announcing his intention to erase the taint of Joan's alleged witchcraft from his historical slate. Judges were appointed and hearings were held. But what started in Charles's self-interest actually became a trial to clear Joan's name.

On and off for six years (1450–1456), Joan's friends and foes volunteered and were summoned to testify. Childhood friends, soldiers, banner-bearers, priests, family, and the nobility eagerly spoke on her behalf. Witnesses came from near and far asking to be heard.

Of the sixty assessors at her original trial, twenty were summoned. They all swore that they had only been carrying out orders.

Cauchon had died and had been buried with pomp and ceremony, but when officials found that he had at one time cheated Rome of sizeable sums, they exhumed his body and threw it into a sewer. His goal of becoming the archbishop of Rouen had never been realized. No one would testify in his behalf at the trial of rehabilitation.

Guillaume Erard, who had denounced Joan at the cemetery at Saint Ouen, was dying the slow death of leprosy and could not testify.

Joan's mother pleaded before the officials at Notre Dame in Paris that they clear Joan's memory. She lived to hear the archbishop of Rheims, on July 7, 1456, acknowledge that Joan's original trial had been wicked, and he publicly restored Joan to the church. Isabelle d'Arc died in 1458, having lived on a pension given by the grateful city of Orléans for her daughter's bravery. Joan's father had died of grief shortly after the tragedy at the stake.

Joan's brother Jean succeeded Baudricourt as captain of Vaucouleurs barracks. Her brother Pierre moved to Orléans.

Priests Isambard and Ladvenu volunteered as witnesses for the hearing to clear Joan's name, and they confessed their shame and fear regarding her original trial.

Jean d'Estivet, a prosecutor at Joan's trial, had been drowned (possibly murdered) by the time the trial of rehabilitation was held.

Durand Lassois, the uncle who had supported Joan without doubt, lived to testify in her behalf.

When the rehabilitation trial ended, Joan was declared to be without sin of body or soul, and two ceremonies marked the public declaration. One was held at Saint Ouen cemetery, where Joan had been forced to recant, the other in the market square where she had been burned at the stake.

As the years passed, the Duke of Alençon, who had served Joan in battle, was condemned to life imprisonment in a tower of the Louvre, convicted of secret correspondence with the English. Later he was exonerated.

La Tremoille was put in prison at Chinon as a traitor to France.

Louis de Contes became lord of Novyon and of Reugles.

D'Aulon was made a town official in Beaucaire. He had supported Joan all the way from Vaucouleurs to the stake.

Charles VII lived to see the English run from Paris in November, 1437, within the time that Joan had predicted it would happen. By 1450, the English had lost their foothold in Normandy. By 1453, they were gone from French soil. It is said that Charles referred to Joan as he lay dying, but no one knows for sure that this was so. His death came on July 22, 1461.

The Church of Saint Saviour, which hovered over the tragedy in the Rouen market square, is gone, but the market is still there.

For years Rouen hung its head in shame for its place in history. Only after one hundred years did it erect a marker, and two hundred years later it placed a statue of

Joan, not at the old market, but at a designated circle called Place de la Pucelle. Today there is a statue of her in the Rouen cathedral.

Two small plaques on a wall of the archbishop's palace in Rouen read:

In this Archiepiscopal Palace
On Tuesday, the 29th of May, 1431
was held the sitting of the process
of
Joan of Arc
At which she was cited to appear next
morning at the Old Market.

In this Archiepiscopal Palace
On Wednesday, the 7th of July, 1456,
The Cardinal d'Estouteville being
Archbishop of Rouen
Was delivered the sentence of
the rehabilitation
of Joan of Arc.

In 1456, Pope Calixtus III pronounced Joan innocent. In 1875, the question of her canonization as a saint was first discussed in Rome. In 1909, Pope Pius X pronounced her beatification, the first step toward canonization. On May 9, 1920, five hundred years after her death, Pope Benedict XV pronounced Joan the Maid of Orléans to be Saint Joan. On July 10, 1920, the French government proclaimed the day of her death, May 30, a national holiday.

Chronology

1412	January 6, born in Domrémy Parish, Lorraine Province, France
1424	First hears the voices
1428	July, leaves Domrémy
1429	Visits Captain de Baudricourt at Vaucouleurs; March, visits the Dauphin at Chinon Castle; May 8, victory in Battle of Orléans; July 17, Dauphin crowned King Charles VII of France
1430	May 24, Joan captured at Compiègne
1431	February 21, trial begins in Rouen; May 30, dies at the stake, Rouen
1450	Trial of rehabilitation begins
1456	July 7, pronounced innocent by Pope Calixtus III
1909	Beatified by Pope Pius X
1920	May 9, declared a saint by Pope Benedict XV in Rome

Chronology

Bibliography

Buchan, Alice. *Joan of Arc and the Recovery of France.* New York: The Macmillan Company, 1948.

Buxton, Ethel Mary. *Jeanne d'Arc.* Philadelphia-New York: J. B. Lippincott Co., 1914.

Close of the Middle Ages, The. Cambridge Medieval History, Vol. VIII, pp. 244–251. New York and Cambridge, England: The Macmillan Company, 1936.

Dickler, Gerald. *Man on Trial, History-Making Trials,* pp. 43–60. Garden City, N. Y.: Doubleday, 1962.

Endore, Guy. *The Sword of God: Jeanne d'Arc.* New York: Garden City Publishing Co., 1931.

Fabre, Lucien. *Joan of Arc.* New York-Toronto-London: McGraw-Hill Book Co., 1954.

Michelet, Jules. *The Life of Joan of Arc.* Chicago: The Spencer Press, 1937.

Monahan, Michael. *My Jeanne d'Arc.* New York and London: The Century Co., 1928.

Paine, Albert Bigelow. *Joan of Arc: Maid of France,* Vol. II. New York: The Macmillan Company, 1925.

Purcell, Mary. *The Halo on the Sword.* Westminster, Maryland: The Newman Press, 1952.

Rankin, Daniel and Claire Quintal. *The First Biography*

of Joan of Arc. Pittsburgh: The Pittsburgh Press, 1964. Winwar, Frances. *The Saint and the Devil.* New York and London: Harper and Bros., 1948.

INDEX